POETRY THAT SINGS

VOLUME ONE
Featuring
THE FIRST BLACK PRESIDENT

C. J. JACKSON

iUniverse, Inc.
New York   Bloomington

POETRY THAT SINGS
VOLUME ONE Featuring THE FIRST BLACK PRESIDENT

iUniverse books may be ordered through booksellers or by contacting:

iUniverse
1663 Liberty Drive
Bloomington, IN 47403
www.iuniverse.com
1-800-Authors (1-800-288-4677)

Because of the dynamic nature of the Internet, any Web addresses or
links contained in this book may have changed since publication and
may no longer be valid. The views expressed in this work are solely those
of the author and do not necessarily reflect the views of the publisher,
and the publisher hereby disclaims any responsibility for them.

ISBN: 9781-4401-3147-9 (pbk)
ISBN: 9781-4401-3148-6 (ebk)

Printed in the United States of America

iUniverse rev. date: 5/8/2009

Contents

ACKNOWLEDGMENTS

I like to first give thanks to God for life and all of the many blessing he so gratefully restored upon me. This series of poems and short stories wouldn' t be possible without the contributions of the following people: My Brother Oscar Jackson, who have been fighting a demon that threaten to take everything he own including his soul. To Tony Williams, as you can see all things are possible with God. A special thank to Joann and Gloria who sat patiently, listen to each and every work and helping by pushing me out of the nest. Without them I wouldn't have anything to prove. To the many street people living in their own world a.k.a. "The Life" and my many co-workers, when I left that world, you all have been my inspiration.

ANOTHER DREAMER

The sixties was a very terrible time in America history, if you were born black, and living in Mississippi; especially Alligator, Mississippi. I was born July 5, 1960 to a mother who was only thirteen and a father that was only eighteen. That's explain why I was passed from one family member to another. Somewhere between the age of one and three years old, I sustain third degree burns on my back and buttock from boiling hot water that slipped out of the hands of my niece. Sometime later, I got an ear infection that made my right ear run continuously. It was not until a couple years later when I moved (what to be the last time, out of many) with my Grandmother (Hattie) that I was taken to a doctor in Shelby, Ms. Dr. Holloway pulled a dead blue blowfly and a large maggot that was very much alive out of my right ear. This may explain why I talk different from the rest of my brothers and sisters. Growing up in my Grandmother house was not a bed of roses either. For starter she had some deep reservation buried down in her subconscious concerning the darker complexion of our race. My older brother and I were the only children that my Grandmother raised. Me being the darkest, brought nothing but pain, shame and the feeling of indifferent. In her mind (may God bless her soul), boys should not bath no more than once a month. Two pairs of trousers were sufficient for a full school term. Stories about the outhouses, the wood burning stoves, days without soap or toothpaste and the many days of going to school with lard on my face and in my hair could fill volumes. Nevertheless, for now digest some words of poetry and if somewhere, a line or two touches your soul, then I have done my job.

STOP DRAGGING ME

Now it came to pass, right before the greatest of all civil wars, blacks got tired of being dragged. From coast to coast, east to west, from the cold north to the UN- thinkable dirty south, blacks stood up and joined together. No longer willing to turn the other cheek, while white policemen and hate groups were killing their brothers and sisters and dragging them all about in the street.

They began to form hate groups of their own. Now white people were killed and their homes, churches and schools were being burned. And just like that the Federal Government stepped in with martial law, declaring that the Black Panther have returned.

If we the people, supposedly being of a God fearing society, don't want this reality to be; then we much declare war on all hate groups and Police Officers who have the same agenda. You know it very sad when I think about my United States Of America, you sat back with binder on, while a different Hate Group pop up on the Internet every week, teaching the young out there to hate as they do. But right now you want do nothing, but just wait until we form our own Hate Groups, that's when you will come up with your fallacious propaganda design to hide the hands of those who threw the first rock. So you tell me how am I suppose to act, when you are disrespecting, beating and shooting me down all because I am black? For most of you, it was people who looked like me that rear you and that a fact. Most of your assess was obtained through generation of tears, pains, and sweat right off my ancestors back. I guess, I shouldn't be too hard on you, for you are only the fruit off the tree. As with everything and everybody, there's some good fruits and some bad fruits.

For all of you who just setting back and watching, not bother because it don't directly affect you, or you feel it not your concern. Just remember chickens always come back home to roost, then it is your turn. We are all the colors of the rainbow. Look up it is beautiful can't you see? Your blood is red as mine, but for right now, you have the power to stop disrespecting, beating, killing and dragging me.

ROCK MAN

From dust to dawn, between sun bright and moonlights,
I take familiar steps to an out-of-date tune.
Whether sweeping the hall o r painting the jail house wall,
day after day I'm reminded of how I took my fall.
Brother this, brother that, some real, some fake, please give, please
take. I feel no pain nor do I play any games.
I'm about the business of known all.
I don't have to perpetrate the fraud.
I know few and then many most without a name.
To know me is to learn me. I'm just the rock man.
    Pick up a tray or pass a tray with eyes of an hawk and ears of
an eagle, this kid knows his way.
I'm down for drugs but that not all.
I smile and talk light, not a preacher but I learn to check without a
fight.
A fool will beef and a sucker will weep.
    Now I can't enjoy many of life pleasure cause being locked
up hurt more than
you can measure.
I used to play ball by robbing Paul.
Now I lie to Fred just to feed Red.
An unheard lie is the one that they will tell after I'm dead.
From Inmates to good Officers even those on the take, my friends I
can count on one hand and they all call me the Rock Man.

I'M THE MAN IN THE MIDDLE

In the center of two women, that's where you're find me.
Playing one against the other, fighting among themselves.
Me dodging the mud, riding through the midst of discombobulating
and insanity is where I like to be.
    Don't quote a string of my hair; cause when you step to me,
I don't know you, never seen you and definite never promise to meet
you anywhere. My tongue is like that of a snake.
I 'll swear up and I'll swear down.
But if you turn me upside, you couldn't count the lies that would hit
the ground.
    I'm always looking for another woman to take.
You can;t break my heart by leaving me.
Yes I kiss your lips, sucked your tongue, even closed my eyes and
screamed out your name, guess what? It was all fake.
    Unlike Jody I'm true to the game.
Candy licking is how I earned my name.
So don't trust me with your friend or your baby-sitter, because as sure
as the sun come up in the morning, I'll still be the man in the middle.

BETTY

As in the inflating of a balloon, my pulse continually to rise.
Blinded by infatuations, I lost my foothold, for I was captivated by
her style.
Her lips were juicy and her tongue begging mine to come inside.
      My lips parted themselves as I watch her with my eyes.
The swag of her hips made me exhale harder with each breath, as I
watch the sugar coated, honey dripping of words fall from her lip.
I'm imagining tasting the spices as I roll her tongue together with
mine. Back and forth, up and down, from side to side and all around.
My tongue dipping in and darting out.
No longer able to keep my eyes open, therefore, I close them,
as I felt my heart tearing away at my chest.
      I began to make sounds of moans that were unfamiliar to me.
My legs have become stranger as I struggle to inhale bit of air,
I manage to steal off her cheek.
Betty began to moan, as she tried to pull away,
the harder she pulled, the more she would moan, and the harder
I held on.

TO MY MOTHER, NO BODY CARE

Oh mother of passion, where are you? Two brain surgeries and a triple
by-pass, tubes taped to my nose and arms, what am I to do?
Lying here with that famous stare, you know the one, when life isn't
fair. Your son is dying and nobody care.
Convicted I was, convict I am.

Aches and pain from multiple wounds. In a suffocated room
with a harden guard, oh mother your son is doom.
coughing, splitting up blood, with a urine bag hanging from my bed,
my upper body is warm but cold are my legs.
He visited me last night and that's a fact.
Coming back to get me, he told me so...standing over there, resentful
dying convict I am and nobody care.

Last night, I dreamed of heat and fire that was too hot to
bare. Don't cry I wasn't along, father was there.
Can't breath mother, my throat is blazing, gone are my esophagus
and my evil ways.
My brain is slowly deteriorating, this life, your son, my focus is
rapidly fazing.
Would say I'm sorry but with one foot in hell it too late.
Damn you mother, and all others that I hate!!!

I will go to hell rather than sit with you and eat off a silver
plate. Now my upper body is cold.
Oh, mother, darkness is everywhere.
I'm sorry, I'm crying, I'm dying and nobody care.

TO MY SON, BROKEN HEART

I confirmed your present before I knew that the richness within my
blood was you.
One morning I did awake to a beat, felt like tiny drums from my
stomach to my feet.
This secret I couldn't keep, doctor came a boy baby said he.
This you're been caring for weeks, time came my wound open and I
did give birth. Eight pounds and seven ounces of pure love you were
my last, but yet my first.
   Years passed and grew you did.
What happen to the teaching and the love I gave?
Aches pain and tears, I did shed. Lord I prayed and lord I cried.
More aches and more pain no matter how hard I tried.
I used to dream of a doctor even a lawyer.
I was such a fool, you see my beautiful son for all of my pain and
tears, you raped and kill before finishing high school.
   I saw you at the state penitentiary.
Gone were by baby and all of my years.
Before me stood a stranger with more sins, only God could recognize
the boy within. As this mother turn and depart; all that left is pain,
sorrow and a broken heart.

DIFFERENT FACES

I can see it coming, like two freight trains bounded for a head on collision. They called it the war of the races, dripping in blood, a great nation fell. Ended with bullet but sparked by bad decision, millions of fathers, sons, mothers and daughters dying.
Can't see their names, just the different faces.
A end is surely near, first was the burning of the churches and the schools, now the killing.
The great one of old and the new is coming.
Winds of many rivers are still, but the blood just keeps on running.
Other nations talking but no one is doing, the great book says out of fear. One eye of the storm was a fool who gave Satan his rights and took prayer out of school. Dead are everywhere in many places.
They couldn't live together the many fathers, mothers, sons, and daughters of this great nation.
I can't see their names, just the dead and dying of both races.

PROCRASTINATION

Dreams are so many, as I sit in thoughts.
Life is like the fading gleam of a super train, whose ticket was never given nor was it brought.
　　　Had i's I should haves, if I had, dancing inside my head.
For my perpetually sorrow, I have only a tear.
God be my witness, here I lay for all to see and hear.
In my book of life, under work, show nothing more than had i's, I surely must be dead.
　　　Things so many have I tried, skill and knowledge's I took for a ride. God blessed me with a gift, but I don't recognize it.
Motivation, education and determination, all set in the back seat.
Riding high up front were had i's, I should have, if I had, they all were my meat.
On this procrastination of life, gone are my many dreams or were they all lies?

THE FIRST BLACK PRESIDENT

Fear not O Great Mystery Babylon.
Like the boy king born in Bethlehem,
the seed of your ancestors is at hand.

  Through divine intervention, he cried out in the wilderness,
with the voice of a thousand roaring waterfalls, saying;
"what was first shall be last", "what was first shall be last",
therefore go and possess the land.

  Hearing the familiar call, another dreamer answer.
Like others before, he too a descendant of slaves.
Roads to the Great House never painless.
But for his progeny, he had to, although the hurt was substantially
insurmountable.
Between the masses, lines were drawn, detached by pigmentation,
gender even homes.

  World great power stood motionless as oppressors and
oppressed conceivably rolled over in hell.
The four winds, the Might Mississippi River even Father Time did
ceased and the God's held their breath.

  The truth that the Founding Fathers spoke of, if God be just
and we know he is; for our horrendous sins, what is to become of us?
The Goat, Dragon, Serpent and their followers reviled with swift
tongues. "Save Babylon", "Save Babylon", "Save Babylon".

  From the highest mountain, Martin yelled down, "stay
strong, be firm and continually to vote".
Picking his self up from the dust, the descendant of slaves had the
audacity to hope.
Through blood, sweat, tears and dying; while standing on Martin's
shoulder the formal slaves did rise.
Just like Martin, they too could finally see the prize on the other side.

LIFE OF A TRUCKER

Lying flat on the top bunk, I looked up; all about me was my best
friend. Gone were the many suspicious slaps on the back.
A reading light and the sound coming from her speaker made me grin.
The family and few friends I thought I had, except from them,
the hundreds of miles apart, even then while being all along I'm
sometimes glad.

      The freight liner of mine, she's something else; you'll see.
Only I have the keys to her heart, and no-one turn her on but me.
A home away from home, no better money maker you;re fine.
Down the many highways and by-ways, her CB and radio, what
beautiful music they make.
Her steering feel good to my hands.
When I'm lost she even tell me what direction to take.

      TV, VCR, Refrigerator and Microwave, you know I enjoy all
of her.
Up the hill, down the hill, back to and from, another dollar been made.
A favorite I ask of none, well...maybe just one, sing for me;
"Life Of A Trucker, as we faze".

ONLY I KNOW HIS NAME

In my town up on a hill where I live, sat a crazy man.
Keep over five thousand dollars in his pocket.
Say he's hunted by bad memories of a dead wife, who picture he wear
around his neck in a locket.
        Every day he sat and talk, same spot, same time, prefer
talking to himself, since no-one else is worthy.
I found him to be a little presumptuous, but definite a straight up
guy.
His conversation was out of this world, kept me speechless, captivated
by words, my mind was beyond the sky.
No-one knows from where he came, this personification of a genius, a
master of dialect and "only I know his name.

DAMAGE PROPERTY

Just like the Northern Wind of cold, I the Traveler, continually so boldly.

The distant I traveled from East to West, then from North to South, I find to be the same.

Not noticeable at first, the scars of battle, with wounds running deep, the pain is all I gain.

I did try another, she was a mother, lonely I detested but it was love that betrayed me.

      The apple of my eyes was not to be.

Victimized by past love; the tears I fought, swearing by day, crying at night, emptiness and the guilt of shame was mine by right.

AND I WALK WITH HIM NO-MORE

As the raging wind of a storm blew all around;
the house that my Father and I build seen destine to be blown down.
Down upon my knees, I begged for mercy, forgiveness with a heart
full of resentfulness, I pleased with God not to tear us a part.

      Trimming in fear, tears screaming down my face, I asked for
heaven sake, throwing all of my cards on the table; I prayed to my
God my soul not to take.

      As quickly as it begin, the wind did cease.
The darkness turned into light and the sun began to shine, through
this my house and I was safe.
The food, the wine, the women, oh! What a feast? I forgot my prayers
and the Good Book, I threw it against the door, and I walked with
him no-more.

HIS LAST MEAL

In this world, the best things in life I'll been told, are free.
But from just one pay check from losing everything, a monster of my own creation has returned; and like fire on wood, my pet is trying to consume me. Now that I'm no longer employed, my financial burden has matured. Even now as I write, my pet is on a secret mission of search and destroy, code name Mike.

Faith I'll been told small as a grain of muster seed, can move mountains. Yes, I;m scare, but this fear I must tell you is not just for me, but for my family. See I have two little girls and then a son that I have not seen in years. A long way, I have came, but somewhere and somehow, I'll gotten off the beaten path.

I can see the smallest of insects now that my horse has run from under me. God I cried, Lord I have prayed that you remember your lost child, and forgive me for feeding a pet that incline to believe that it getting a deal by making his master his last meal.

SLOW RAIN

Misty, drizzling and damp this rain.
Cloudy are her skies bring undue fogs upon the earth.
This day, I knew it would come, a friend has passed, today is bury,
your work must be done.
Like death is to birth, she has no more to gain, but the dirt upon her
face and the falling of slow rain.
       I remember her smile as I waved good-bye.
Her eyes, sparked, dancing with the lights as she speedy away.
She arrived home on time, just to meet death.
All dressed in black he smiled, told her not to worry another day.
Taking her into his arms he kissed her.
As he sucked her last breath, remembering of family and friends
brought tears screaming down her face.
She wiggles and coughed trying hard to push him away.
But mightily was his strength and steadfast was his plains, couldn't
put them off for another day.
       How sad this day of pain, with lights on bright, cars of family
and friends
did pass.
Your funeral I didn't attend, afraid of losing my cool among men.
How sweet your smile, beautiful memory I hope will last, your dying
makes today your time to shine.
Here I sat in my lonely room, wiggling in pain, as I watch the falling
of slow rain.

WHY DID I HAVE TO BE A FOSTER CHILD?

At an young age, my parents turn their back; giving me up for no reason other then the fact that I was young, ill looking and very, very black.

Traveling from house to house, East to West, mostly North to South. Starved and hungry but the angry inside forced me sometimes to go without.

Daily rain of tears ran freely down my face, as the memories of my Father penetrating my innocent.

A scene so real that the blood, I can almost smell.

A cry for help, what's seen like the thousands times, Mom finally looked up. Her eyes red, focused on a rock that turned out to be nothing but bread.

As her head dropped back down to her chest, my pain became so unbearable, that I blacked out and God only knows what my Father done next.

I'm all grown up now, but the past still had a hold on me.

Daddy is in jail and Mom is so strong out on drugs, that her present I rather not see.

Can't keep a man friend, them, I never learn to trust.

My body goes stiff, numb, and cold just from the touch.

I turn to women whom I frequently abuse.

Filling them with hurt and pain, makes me feel good that it them instead of me, that's being used.

Tried to kill myself several times.

Cut my body from my neck down to my stomach.

Doctors sew me up and sent me home, telling the policemen that something is wrong.

To hell with her mind, they said; a few years in jail and she's be fine.

I'm fifty-one and I still dream of a nice home with a nice family and flowers by the miles.

But in reality my world is a living hell.

Demons trying to process my soul.

Mama why did I have to be a foster child?

THE OTHER NIGHT

In front of my cell sat an Officer watching my every move.
Cell block Two-G, yes that's me I'm Mike, during hard times, they
say I'm paying my dues.
Rag, Dirty Red and Neck Bone, yea my cell buddies are really cool.
Just the other night, Dirty Red and Rag stagged a fight.
The Officers ran and spray their gases.
When the commotion ended and the gas settles, Neck Bone and I
gave each other high fives.
We didn't care if it was wrong or right, the only enemy I ever known
ate his meal, drank his water, his last, just happen to be the other night.
      Ling on my back in my cell I often think of yesterdays and
the day before about you.
You're so fine with me doing times, a girl so pure with breath so fresh,
the taste of mint come to mind.
But wait before you're out of my sight, what about my children?
Oh yea, that's right, I mess that up too, just the other night.
      I was short dog, doing short time for a dime.
Now I'm standing on my head because Dirty Red is dead.
Rag introduced a neat trick, for time already served, the Brother
pulled a switch.
I'm down to a week and a wake-up, God I do believe.
Damn! A monkey wrench out of no-where; for ten to twenty Neck
Bone copped a plead.
The one-eight-seven was smooth, not a witness in sight, well, not
until the other night.

THIS WORLD AIN'T BOUT NOTHING

As if passing out candy, that judge gave me fifteen years.
Time stood still; a curse word formed in my mind.
I swallow a hard lump of something as I fought back the tears.
Cut down in prime, for being young and foolish.
Like a sinking ship, helpless, I'm caught in a vice.
The judge looked me straight in my eyes, his words cutting like a knife,
as he reminded me; this day being the first day of the rest of my life.
          Life I'll been told is a game, I played it and I played it well.
Gone is my fame, unlike many I'll take all of my medicine myself, I
won't give up any names, when we meet down in hell, I'll have a few
more stories to tell of how I took my fall and landed in jail.
These four walls, bars and doors slamming all the time, make me
want to kill or hurt somebody.
Sometimes I wake up and think, today, I should just knock the mess
out of one of these policemen.
But I just laid the Good Book down and I remember God words
saying this world ain't bout nothing

I'M AFRAID OF YOUR IGNORANT MISGUIDED CRAZY LOVE

So it come down to this, out relationship as lover and cohabitants can
no longer assist.
You're not trusting me to talk or to be friend with the object sex,
without the pointed finger and accusing eyes subjecting a steamy
heated night of passion, filled with animated raw sex.
Birds, no matter what color or flavor can never be more eloquent
as two turtle doves, nor can I be happy or see a future with your
ignorant misguided crazy love.
　　　　When we first met, the future looked so clear and bright.
That was before your self-pity, low self-esteem, jealous, hurt, pain and
tears steaming from a past broken heart came to light.
You're first to enter the house and star sixty-nine or check the caller
ID, then you cast suspicious eyes at me before asking question about
the name and number that unfamiliar to you or me.
Nor day or night go by without you checking my clothes, and what
process you to smell my underclothes, only God knows.
　　　　You say you're leaving me because I'm a cheat, liar, and no-
good low-down dirty mother sucker.
This my house; I have begged you to get out.
All you do is slam doors, break windows and glasses but won't talk.
I'll settle for a peace of mind, I'm not looking for another.
You call my job to see if I;m at work.
You call to see, have I left work.
You call home and once you hear my voice you quickly hang up the
phone. I had the police to throw you out, to keep from hitting you in
your mouth.
You're used to being beaten, called me a punk because I want give
you what you're looking for.
Even told you to your face that I have someone else.
Your action let me know what you're all about.
God knows from heaven above I'm sick and tired, but more than
that; I'm afraid of your ignorant misguided crazy love.

THE WAY SHE WALK

Shake it up; shake it down, keeping m head turning all around.
Do tell; is it for someone else or is it for me?
If I be that lucky then all of it I much see.
I'm too old to play games beside it just never been my thing.
The way you move really pain my heart.
You make me feel that rush; even when we'll miles apart.
A truer lover you never find, one that knows how to make love to
your mind as well as your body.
Then again, I like the way you talk, especially the way she walk.

TURNING EVERY HOURS INTO A PAY DAY

Since you asked before, well; it about time to let you know, just what time it is so you can stop sweating me every time you see me out in the field.

For a sawbuck, I;m doing time, but with eyes wide open to God shining light he enlighten my mind.

You see in my cell I once rebel, and just like a fool and his money will soon depart, I'm pushing pen to paper, not taken names just busting heart. I once was lost until God showed me the way.

So now I', turning seconds into minutes, minutes into hours and every hour into a pay day.

You may think it silly but before I came to jail I was a wilily. Shacking here, peeping there, trying to get somewhere without paying the fare.

Now I'm a family man known all over the land, no longer a player of the night, just a black brother trying to do what right.

My children can be proud when they say Dad did it his way, by turning failure into success, cents into dollars and making every hour into a pay day.

THE ART OF MASTURBATION

As the reflection of the moonlight creep across my face, for the things
I do while lying in bed; I could easily be charged with a rape case.
I'm engaged in this crazy act of love making and I can't seen to stop
because it involve giving as well as taking.

      Physically you stacked the cards making yourself both
unwillingly and unable.
But mentally I switch the deck, now I make love to you at will.
All through out the house even on top and under the kitchen table.

      You see physically I don't want or need you and I could never
reach my peak cause you wouldn't know what to do.
Whether it is my freakish ways or just freakish by natural, you could
never comprehend my extraordinary taste.

      While watching you walking across the street I made a
picture image of you from the top of your head to the bottom of your
feet. That night I kissed, sucked and licked your body as I slowly,
mentally pull away the sheet.

      Been abused and hurt so many times, that when you say that
you love and begin to touch me; I just close you out of my mind.
But when I'm all along in my bed room, my finger and hands come
alive, gently touching and squeezing your body, dancing to a mental
tune.

      Sometime I make love to you other times to a total strangle,
some marriage and some not.
When I'm reaching my peak and the star cluster began to bust all
around me, I beg you or make you beg me not to stop.
You see I rape you all the times, sometime over and over again.
But don't get mad, it just happen to be a freakish situation better yet,
why don't you join me in the art of masturbation.

THEY CALL ME NURSE'S AIDE

Like a princess dressed in white, arriving on a smile of sunshine, not just doing the day but throughout the night.
Scented with the fragrant of roses, no colors, creed or illness do I mine.
Even give a big wink when you scratchy my hoses, no better caretaker will you fine.
I'm never over paid, but when there's a problem I'm first to blame.
Yet I lift, clean, roll and wipe, knowing all my patients by name.
I'm a professional, but they call me nurse's aide.
      I dance sing even shouted when you won bingo.
I read to you , laughed with you and encouraged you when you were too afraid to let go.
Listen to you talk while you were angry at time wiping away your tears.
For in me you have entrusted your deepest darkest fears.
Brought your favorite foods, books, and toys, remember that homemade malt?
Yes I done thing to keep you happy that I shouldn't have, like looking away when you added extra salt.
This is your home I am your servant.
Still I will lift, clean roll and wipe, you're have it made.
I'm a professional, but they call me nurse's aide.
      I rejoiced when you arrived and cried when you left.
My stomach is always in a ball of knots.
For the feeling I cannot block.
Sadness took over, when they said no need to feed.
As I peep through your eyes I held your hands and fell to my knee,
with the fading of your last breath I prayed to God your soul to keep,
      But when death took over I was the first to see.
Yet I lifted, cleaned, rolled and wiped.
As I packed your belongings, I fought back the tears with all o f my might.
Told your family how beautifully you went away and your memory I will keep each day because, I'm a professional, but they call me nurse's aide.

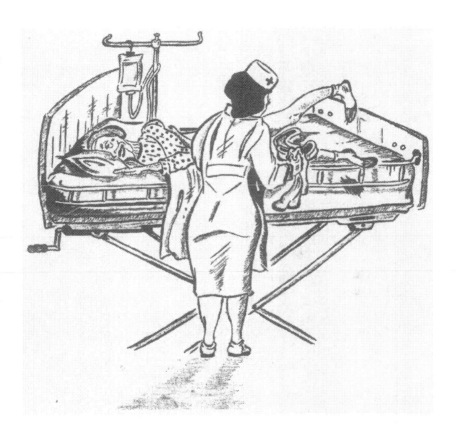

MY DEAR FRIEND

Do you realize that this year is almost gone, and not once have you set foot in my church or falling upon your knee to give thank for the many flowers, birds or trees.

Yesterday when you awoke, you awaken angry for no reason other than it was six in the morning and you felt that it was too early to wake up.

I shook you only to show you the beautiful sunrise, thinking that it would bring amazement and joy to your eyes.

But you cursed the sun and on your face was a frown instead of a smile.

I love you so much that I laid down my own life so that you could have life ever lasting.

You brought tears to my eyes as I watching you set down with your family to eat.

Not once did you give thanks for the many items, not even the meat.

It difficult not to become jealous as I watch you cash your pay checks.

Your blood pressure goes up and your heart beat oh so fast.

I closed my eyes in disbelieves and asked my Father how could this be?

I can't believe that you could care more for your money and that you would actually choose a paper God over me.

Angry at time I may be, but I love you even after your last breath.

I will always give you my very best.

To know me, is to know the Father.

To know the Father, is to know the Son.

Come to me, all who labor and are heavy laden and I will give you rest. From your loving friend Jesus, the only ticket to success.

NEW WORLD ORDER

Land of milk and honey;
the world melting pot, won't last.
Can't be lame, to get money, got to play the game.
Six by six by six, one World Government, coming fast.
　　　　Looking up reluctantly, eyes widen, mouth open, my mind
sigh. Throat choked, watching the sun, moon and stars.
Heart running, blood frozen the hairs on my neck standing.
All bodily function involuntary, many strange things in the skies.
　　　　Countries all talking, can't comprehend,
despaired, afraid of the raging tides.
Darkness so much uncommonly during daylight.
I see soldiers too many to count.
What was hot is now cold and vice versa.
To eat, to sleep, in short to live.
They stamped my number; I crapped out with one roll of the dices.
　　　　Have mercy; give me death I begged for some escape.
Death for me was angry, it wouldn't come.
Super hot rocks falling from the sky.
Mother earth burning, she;s flooding, she;s freezing.
People killing, people running to no-where.
Animal turning, unknown diseases, everywhere is hell; a perfect
storm.
　　　　This new Government, original constitution suspended.
The massive are afraid, need a number to buy anything.
What is happening?
Too much! Too much! Too much of everything.
The killing, the blood pouring down like rain.
Something is in the air; space has lost it power, stuff falling from the sky,
finally a calm. In the cloud, I can hear sweet music, I stood the course.
Still afraid, yet my faith was strong.
Felt my salvation was near, as I rejoiced, I bath in the sun rays,
awaiting the Son Of Man to appear.

FORTY ACRES AND A MULE

Damned if I say it.
Damned if I don't.
Some will hear, and some won't.
Looking into the mirror, reflecting beams of frustrations, angry and stress.
Been three hundreds and ninety years since the first slave ship docked.
Through countless murders, rapes and beating even Babylon's First
Black President, the personification of the American Black Man is still
in a mess.
       Special Field Orders Number Fifteen, made us a promise.
On that tip, gladly we rushed to war.
Losing eyes, limbs some dying, worthy sacrifices.
Freemen hopes of processing lands, in pursuit of a better life at a
higher price.
       Fought bravely and glory.
Became both Officer and Gentlemen.
Returned tired, staved and sick.
Memories of the Emancipator promise; the thought burning through
the spirit like fuel.
       Black Family rejoiced in celebration of the American Dream.
Proud owner of forty acres and a mule.
By a bullet the Emancipator was killed.
Tragically lost of life, a great man died.
       The shot killed the president, including the dreams of many.
Dead was the man and so was his bill.
Mr. Johnson, a bigot by nature, prohibited people that was property,
becoming owners of properties.
Reneged upon, our lands repossessed, no-hope, no-dream,
no-restitution, no-reparation.
       Don't worry be happy, a Black President, what more could
they want?
Easy question when your family stole robbed and took.
Let the past die, you say; Blacks rewards; keep looking to the sky.
The past is never dead, while White's and Others, here on earth,

enjoy their ice-cream, cake and pie.

President Reagan, paid Japanese American twenty thousand each for their internment during the war.

Native American compensated for land.

The Blacks were robbed of past, hopes and future.

Generation gone, memories lost forever.

Taught to love you and hate me.

The angry reflecting from the mirror is the fuel.

How dare you, piss on me, concerning my question about my Forty Acres And A Mule?

OBAMA
THE FIRST BLACK PRESIDENT

Bodies of people, from sea to shinning sea.
The world await, many traveled thousand of miles to see.
Even the God's in heaven, held back thunders and lighting that
we mortals could watch Obama on TV.
       My spirit is high.
I smile widely and brightly from the thought;
America indeed, elected someone Black like me, Commander In
Chief.
With blood pumping crazy, tears unstoppable, my heart flustering.
The tingling sensation of something good felt all over my body.
Oh my! Oh my! Oh my!
       Now I too, feel more American, although many of you
still hate my color.
But his pictures will plastic my walls and through his face my kids
will dream.
Obama, United State's First Black President, only the sky is the limit,
endless possibilities is what this mean.
       Many Whites will retaliate.
Hate Groups multiplying all over the land.
Don't want changes to come, keep the old way, definite not those
Blacks in power.
Wall Street will sink to an all time low.
Just to make him look bad, keep America in a recess.
You're keep the stock market down, even some Governors will hurt
their own States.
They know, any improvements in the economic will make him look
good.
Forget about his character.
Forget about his intelligent.
Forget how eloquently he speaks.
A Black Family in the White House, no joke, not funny, don't laugh,
this is for real and not Hollywood.

Some so angry, they moved away and out.
Thinking, no-one but red blooded, blue eyes White American can run this country.
Wake up people before it's too lake.
The Alpha and Omega, spoke of; "what was, shall be again".
        "Those last shall be first".
"Those down shall rise up".
The great power of God is what this is all about.

OH HURRICANE KATRINA

Oh Katrina I thought you a spoil brat.
The way you sat, watching, waiting, pacing before coming ashore.
Now I know that you were warning all non-believes, you're not like
other before.
Oh Katrina, your voice was screaming "last call", "last chance".
Get out! Please leave now! You don't know me.
You slowly counted down, 10, 9, 8, 7, 6, 5, 4, 3, 2, 1, 0, and Blast Off!!!
After many hours of waiting going from East to West then North to
South, you said time up; let;s dance!!!
        Oh Katrina, as you spring forward from the mouth of the
Gulf, you spit out baby tornadoes as an entrée.
Your winds sent ragging tidal waves as a main course.
Cutting off electricity trapping victims in their places.
In darkly reality is and panic did set in, the look of death frozen on
their faces.
Your eye peeked down at the many vehicles lined the roadway, you
growled; too late, enough is enough!!!
        Oh Katrina, you said fools; how dare you try and test me.
Picking up vehicles, houses, and other structures like toothpicks.
You shattered them, taking babies, women and children's straight out
of strong men arms.
        You released the floodgates of hell, with severe loss of life and
property damage.
Shows how cruel and deadliest you could be.
Left no doubt in anybody mind, now this the whole world could see.
        Oh Katrina, as you past over the aftermath, a fitting history
book. The stink of death was everywhere.
For dessert your rain and rivers trapped victims in, and their would
be savors out.
Through holes in their roof tops some did survive.
The weak and sick died sitting in chairs, some while lying in bed.
Dead decaying bodies, swollen, covered with flies and maggots flowed
down the streets. Bouncing off objects, stopping for viewing, before
continually on a perpetually journey.

Men, women, and children crying; old and young banded together
for the world to see.
The shock of horror and fear causes urinating and others body
functions to run free.
Enemies and foes, blacks, and whites, for a time were as one, prayed
openly, for God to have mercy on me.

Oh Katrina, you cribbed F.E.M.A. And the Red Cross wasn't
ready.
A president was lost for words.
Before the blame game, Governors and Mayors screaming for help,
telling their people to hold steady.

National Guard Soldiers, away in a strange land in hot sand,
under hail of bullets, crying for love one and their States.
Some losing their own life, worrying if family members were alive, if
help was coming and how long it would take.
Back home, unbelievable sadism, cruelty without warning.
Many Peace Officers left before the storm, so the black anarchy went
unchecked, the fear, it own storm, how daunting?

No-one was safe, it was like every scum on earth looked to
murder, rob and rape.
People so dismayed and sadism refused to wait in lines, started to
urinating and defecating on shelter floors.
Shooting and robbing the same people trying to save life.
This cruel and senseless behavior, we cried out; please somebody,
anybody, who would listen, this is still America.
People murdering, robbing, raping, dying of starvation, thirst and
heat exposure, what is this all about?

Oh Katrina, first time in history, turned a portion of paradise
liking a third world country.
Those who life you spared, know that your statement rang true; no
country great or small, or people no matter how rich and powerful
you may think you be, your world upside down, I'll turn.
Kill, mangled, make orphans, separate, and make willows, in fraction
of a split second, you're be A Refugee, A Refugee, A Refugee.
Left with nothing but your own life; you're thanks thee, thanks thee.

WHY DO WOMEN CHOOSE THE WRONG MEN TIME AND TIME AGAIN?

My name is Diann Moore, and you can call it a flaw in my character. But deep down inside, I still want to be Daddy little girl. My Dad was a no-nonsense, hard, roughneck man. I idolized him because he was king of his world. He was a alcoholic, abusive to women and emotionally, physically, unavailable to my mother. But my Dad could talk. He didn't have anything close to perfect English. But he could talk the sweetness out of sugar. I remember him saying once, that if you say what a person want to hear, most of the time you can get what you're asking for.

It was kind of odd when I think about how Dad dominated my mother. In a conversation he never would come right out and tell her to shut up. But whenever she would come close to crossing that line of being disrespectful, he would give her the eye. And that was all that it took to silent her or us. Sometimes she would catch him cheating. She even knew some of the girl, who called themselves friends to her that he was cheating with. Now my mother was no dummy, she have a master degree in engineer, but he would break her down and put her back together as if she was a shotgun. My dad had such a enormous influence over my mother, until her self-esteem was in the negative zone. We did not recognize just how much so, until one day, he just walked out the door. After waiting on my father for six month she decided it was time to get on with her life. Just imagine waiting six month on a man who walked out on you. Left you with three children and didn't write or call. Mom, met this guy name George, and she allow him to move in. We were happy at first, but then he turned out to be too easy. George treated my mom like a queen, candy, flowers and dining was a regular thing. Mom wasn't used to that type of treat- ment, so she would start a augment, sometimes accusing him of having an affair, just because he was too nice. Unlike my father George wouldn't fight her and because of this, mom would call him weak or say that he was less than a man. She started going out and cheating on him. I'm going out and find me a roughneck, she would tell him. Finally poor George couldn't take it any more so he moved out. The next guy my mother picked up his name was Dirty Red. Dirty Red didn't have a job, clothes, home or money, but mom fell in love with this man. She loved his dirty drawers. After mom spent her money, and turned Dirty Red into Mr. Clean Red, he started driving all of his women friends around in her car. Staying out all night, coming home with lipstick on his shirt and his underclothes on wrong. Now I may sound crazy when I say this, but mom was happier with Dirty Red then with sweet George. I think that it all boil down to two things, one is low self-esteem and sex. For one ting most women don't want a man that looks better then they do. They don't want a man that's smarter then they are. By having a man who don't look so hot or with a hold lots of intellect, she feel good about herself. But the bottom line of it all, is sex. No matter how much money, how smart or what type of car you drive, if you can drive that woman crazy in the bedroom, you can have one leg or be in a wheel chair, it doesn't matter. If your love making is great, she will pick you up out of that chair and put you to bed. She will work two job if she have to. I don't care if she is the preacher, doctor or lawyer wife, if you can make her hold body trimmer, she will leave them for you and bring you their money, cars and homes.

As a child now that I think back, I remember hearing funny sounds coming from my mother and father bed room. My mother would come out of that room looking like she just went a round with Mike Tyson. Sweat would be every where, their bedroom would be in a mess, and for some reason, when she tried to talk it didn't make sense. A hour or so ago, they were fighting like cats and dogs. Now she got a big smile on her face, holding his hand, walking him to the door telling him to be careful, after giving him one of her biggest wet kisses, knowing fully well that he would be laying that same pipe to some other woman before darkly turn into light.

LIKE A THIEF IN THE NIGHT HE WILL APPEAL

The year two thousand and nine is here, and like a baby grasping for
his first breath of air;
I now stand squarely with one hundred and eighty degrees in front
and the same behind me.
They have tried me once and I was not denied. I stand here and now,
ready to be tried again.
I bare witness to none, but one and I stand at his right hand. The
sword is my choice of weapon. I eat, sleep, act and talk, but I'm more
than a man.

I come as a raging bull to awaken those that been asleep for
over five hundred years.
My heart does not pump blood of pity nor do I come to make peace.
My orders are clear;
wars are fought by the young. Be that of a newly developed plant
when it's leaves unfolded.
I now speak to all who will hear, if you are young with old ideas, then
it is written, you are old. If you are old with new ideas, then you are
young. All that is old had no place in the New World Order. And
through your ignorant, your blood will run freely on that day.

You Antichrist, have shown the world that you are smart,
have met other like me and them you have destroyed. Six by six by six
be your claim. Unlike them, I want ride on the lighting bolt for I will
be on its side will be your name. When all currency cease to assist and
in it place you're introduce the card. In your moment of glorification
you had your feast.
Then an act build upon arrogant for world domination will you
banish your skin with the mark of the beast. With my sword slicing
through the air, and you with your big bombs thundering,
I promise you that the dead in hell will look small compare to the
bodies laying everywhere.
The coming have been for many years, but when three four of the
earth had been destroyed, like a thief in the night will he appeal.

BIG BROWN EYES

Most morning when I awake I think about the dead, the living, the bills and oh yes, the many women.
Their faces twisting in pain, smeared with salted tear traces, from what supposedly been love that was fake, more often than a few ended with a heart break.
The abused road I travel is rotten and this one here is new.
Yet in all four direction the wind is unforgiving and my future smell the same clean through.
This new love I stake my claim.
Yes, you can laugh but don't close the door.
My smell is the same but I swear I never been here before.
Looking deeply into her eyes I watch her as she talked.
Those big brown eyes reflexing a ebony woman of beautiful, tenderness and compassion.
Her breath labor hard with her passion.
From the first to the last day; to know her is magnificent, to hold her is spectacular.
This jewel of God creation is perfect in every way.
My days are never too long nor are my night so short to dismiss this heart felt sensation of joy while she's in my thought, or the smile I just can't hide whenever I look into her big brown eyes.

DEDICATION

There's a little black spot on the sun today,
because your Father, for the last time, closed his loving eyes and
passed away.
Knowing fully well that his untimely departure would hurt, so he
hesitated when he heard his name, but death wouldn't wait.

   He left you and went to his real home, but he didn't leave
you all along.
Yes, your heart maybe troubled, and you can't see for crying from
time to time.
So you have our deepest sympathy and hopes that these words will
bring a little comfort and some peace of mind.

   The one question that's been asked every since the beginning
of time, why?
The answer is God; he is and will always be.
He love you and so do we.

PIMPING AIN'T EASY

So you like the way I live, you know my life style; fine women, cash money, cars, the best of clothes, gold and all that other jive.
But let me pull your coat, without the fake, and give it to you straight about a brother from the back woods of the Mississippi.
You may try to play him cheat, but cash money he make and ain't a woman been born that he couldn't pull or take.
He put the M in acting and called it macking.
Put the F on act and made pimping a matter-of-fact.
Put the D in her drawer and turned her into a dog.
When she fell and hit her head, he thought she was dead; cause she made a slip when she gave his money to a sucker name Red.
Rest, dress my best, every day putting my skills to the test, making pimping a big success.
Now all of you biter and hater who think that his game is lame and a little sleazy, try making over a hundred grands every week then you're know that pimping ain't easy.
        Betty, sweet, tender, dark and lovely, his bottom girl a real mud kicker, top notch money maker.
He copped her just like stealing a horse, threw down all the hay she could eat, comb her hair, washed her back, he even washed her feet.
Smooth the rope across her back, and she never felt any pain but in her sleep she cried out his name.
When they threw him in jail, he didn't yell, he just study their constitution, their laws and their God.
Then one day it hit him like a hammer; the best pimping is done in church.
While they're taking your money, they're talking about staying out of hell.
I know that I will never see my name in lights but remember this, pimps come in many colors.
While you're looking for fame, just dig your hand deeper into your pocket and charge it to the pimping game.

ABOVE THE LAW
AND
WHAT IF?

2000 and 2004 elections was stolen by Bush... AND
WHAT IF?
President Bush and Cohorts planned 9/11... AND
WHAT IF?
President Bush allowed Osama Bin Laden and family to leave the
United States.. AND
WHAT IF?
President Bush knew Iraqis didn't have W.M.D... AND
WHAT IF?
President Bush goals was to kill Saddam Hussein for personal
reason... AND
WHAT IF?
President Bush cause the Military to kill thousand of innocent Iraqis,
women, children's and babies... AND
WHAT IF?
President Bush authorized torturing, although it goes against the
Geneva Convention.. AND
WHAT IF?
President Bush turned a three billions dollars surplus into a three
trillion dollars deficit... AND
WHAT IF?
President Bush planned to suspend the Constitution for person
gain...... AND
WHAT IF?
President Roosevelt said "No man is above the law and no man is
below it, nor do we ask any man permission when we ask him to obey
it"... AND
WHAT IF?
That man is President George W. Bush... AND
WHAT IF?
He thinks he's above the law... AND
WHAT IF?

DEATH

Something born, something died.
Something planted, something uprooted.
A love lost is a love found.
A smile up is a frown upside down.
       Inhale first breath for life.
Exhale last breath for death.
Round strong oak tree is beautiful majestic to behold.
A downed oak tree is the young tree future.
It too, stood tall and proud.
Limbs long, and thick.
Head full of hair before it got too old.
       Instead of joy it bring sorrow.
Every second, every hour always stalking.
Walks eight times around a pregnant woman bed.
Wondering if he should take one or both today,
or save one or both for tomorrow.
       His character is dark and cold.
He is the enemy of longevity.
Plays games with procrastinators.
Love to watch the rich and power try and hold on to life.
His bag of tricks is always within reach..
You're never see him without a full load.

BLACK ON BLACK

Yea yea I'm talking about you.
Mr. and Mrs. over excited, quick to react,
Jump to conclusions, ready to march,
destroying your own neighborhood,
whenever you hear of a cop shooting a black.
You run in head first,
ready to fight, without knowing all of the facts.
             Everyday black on black crimes,
I don't hear a word out your mouth.
Robbing , raping and killing from the ghetto's of the North,
to robbing, raping and killing from the ghetto's of the cotton fields.
Your mentality is black on black crime is normal.
Long as it stays in the blacks part of town, and we are doing it
to ourselves.
In reality it worse when we do it to each other.
When you respect each other everybody else will to.
We disrespect everybody, including our own mother.
             Nothing wrong with Rap.
When done in contexts and respect.
Any intelligent man or woman can express without the curse words
disrespecting females, hyphen drugs money, killing and pushing sex.
What's up with your pant hanging down?
My mother and my woman turns their heads when you come around.
Everybody think you're a clown.
Don't get mad, but this is how you act.
Thinking you're cool, hip, bad and bold
by showing us your crack.

WAYS TO KEEP THE BLACK MAN DOWN

Now let me count the ways, first let's keep him broke and hopeless.
Let's keep him in the dark, hungry, barefoot and crazy.
Let's scrip him of all dignity and pride.
Blindfold him, misguide and set traps for him.
Turn his women folks against him and reprogram his children.
Take away his land, livestocks, and farms.
Close out all assets, accounts, and all real estate transaction.
Let;s take him for a ride, sue him, and take away his child.
We could slander his name, play mind games, and enter him into the
hall of shame.
       Let's love him by pretending to turn the other cheek.
Enter him in a sweepstakes, promising him cars, truck, and jeeps.
Let's opening up casinos in the deep south, you know that they are
more ignorant down there, they're never figure it out.
Why not invent and tell him the half truth about A.I.D.S. And its
beginning.
Let's block his soul by weighing him down in sin.
Shall we? I think we shall, overwork and underpay him, make him
our hero for today.
Why hell, let's play him to the left, by building projects and turning
them into small
ghetto's.
We can send in drugs so deadly and cheat, they're be zombies within
weeks.
Yea guys! Let's get with the program, by promoting hard core Raps,
you know the kind;
your mother is a b---- and f---this and kill that.
Make them disrespect their own mothers.
Man we could put guns out there, those black bastard will start
killing each others for fun.
Let's frame him and keep him in jail.
We could tell him that he's sick, and give him all types of medication.
Boys I'm telling you we could have fun by making their life a living
hell.

Let's genocide them by teaching birth-control, pasting out condoms in schools by the pounds.
Let's take prayer out of school and teach them nothing about themselves except every things
black is bad.
Man there are so many ways, we can keep them down, but the best one of all is to let him help us to keep the black man down.

SATAN

Worship me and I shall set you free, I will grant your wishes and
requests instantly.
Everything you touch will become gold, all I ask in return is your
soul.

I will show you how to fly. I can remove all problems and
pain in a trickle of an eye. None of those commitments will I uphold,
none of that love stuff, just your soul.

You can remain bitter and cold. Not caring, not sharing,
and I'll speak very bold, all I ask in return is your soul. I'll make your
dreams come true, grass greener and everything you touch turn into
gold, just remember all I ask is your soul.

FORGIVE ME

When we got married my love for you was unconditional and my
feeling personalized.
It was the happiest day of my life, when I made you my wife.
Over the years we have grew, you with me and me with you.
Now here wee are at a stumbling block; and you have taken the key
to your heart, and now it is locked.

      We were having problems and at the time seemed impossible
to solve, sometimes during the argument, I would displace myself as
if I wasn't involved.
You have done things, but I won't throw them back in your face, as to
take things off of me so I can win this race.
I have made a mistake, and I want to apologize before it's too late.

      Without you it is useless, for you are one/half of my soul,
and I can't survive with no shelter and be left out in the cold.
You and my girls mean more to me than life itself.
I can't just shew you away like dust on a shelf.
Being human is what I am but that's no excuse, I should have used
good judgment and stood up like a man.
This time I will put wisdom and knowledge's to use, will you please
forgive me?

DREAM WORLD

With ears open and eyes closed; just outside of death and at times, I even snore.

I'm the president of the United States or maybe the high price lawyer that always win the debate.

I have so much money that I own the land of milk and honey.

My people adore me.

They praise me so much that sometimes its bore be.

I'm the jack of all trades, wrote a song that went platinum called, "I Got It Made."

I'm the king and I have a queen with many rings and curls.

I have it all in my dream world.

My wants are never a problem, anything I want, I just dream.

Lately I've acquired my very own basketball team.

Most people work too hard for the things they want; me I just dream. Yesterday I brought myself a diamond cluster ring. Sometimes I fall asleep and forget to dream; that when I loose everything the money, cars and the girls it all gone including my basketball team.